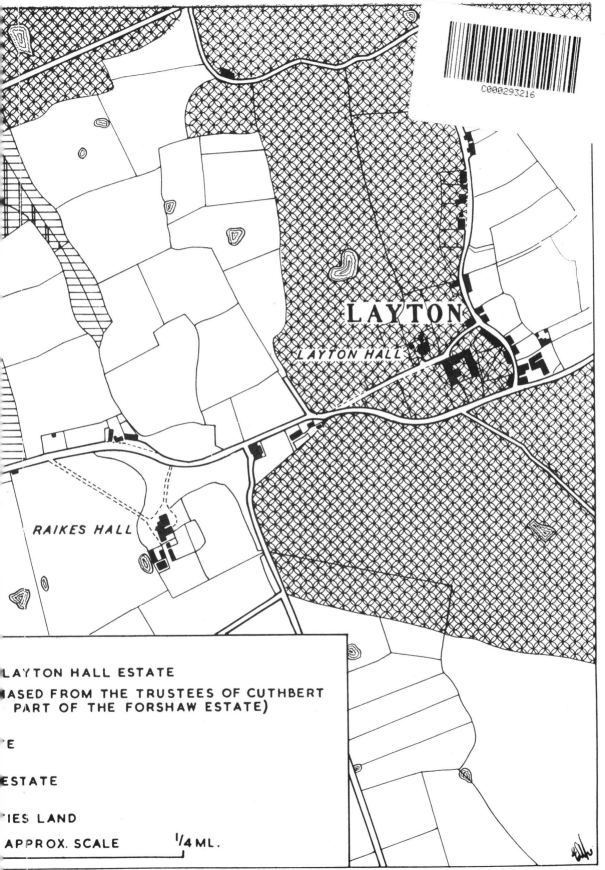

LAYTON

LAYTON HALL

RAIKES HALL

LAYTON HALL ESTATE

ASED FROM THE TRUSTEES OF CUTHBERT
PART OF THE FORSHAW ESTATE)

E

ESTATE

IES LAND

APPROX. SCALE          1/4 ML.

Blackpool in the 1840s showing the principal estates.

# BLACKPOOL
## A Pictorial History

Blackpool at the end of the 19th century.

# BLACKPOOL
## A Pictorial History

## Ted Lightbown

**Phillimore**

1994

Published by
PHILLIMORE & CO. LTD.
Shopwyke Manor Barn, Chichester, Sussex

ISBN 0 85033 910 3

Printed and bound in Great Britain by
BIDDLES LTD.
Guildford, Surrey

# List of Illustrations

*Frontispiece:* Blackpool at the end of the 19th century.

# *Acknowledgments*

I particularly wish to express my gratitude to W. John Smith, F.S.A. for the use of his important collection of early Blackpool material and for his advice and encouragement. I would also like to thank James Burkitt, A.L.A., District Librarian, Martin Ramsbottom and Gillian Marsland, Reference Librarians, and the staff of Blackpool Reference Library. I am indebted to Norman Cunliffe, Alan Stott and Gerry Wolstenholme for reading the text and to the following for their help and co-operation: Max Armstrong of Blackpool Pleasure Beach, Cyril Bloor, Graham Boyes, Zena Burslam, Albert Clayton, Phyllis Dawson, Bob Dobson, William Fisher, John Garnham, Robert Haley, Richard Hardwick, Peter Jackson, Bessie Mather, Peter Owen and the staff of the *Evening Gazette*'s photographic library, Eric Scholes, Barry Shaw, Mark Wheeler of Studio D, Linda Wolstenholme, Walter and Rita Wolstenholme and Allan Wood. Special thanks are due to my wife, Ann, for her great help, forbearance, and the occasional push.

I am grateful for permission to reproduce the following illustrations: Blackpool Pleasure Beach, 163, 165-67, 169, 171, 172; Graham D. Boyes, 40, 54, 58, 60, 77-9, 162; Bob Charnley, 1; Phyllis Dawson, 64, 65; E.G. Round, 2, 22; *Evening Gazette*, 3, 34, 86, 121, 129, 139, 141, 151; John Garnham, 96, 110, 112, 113, 119, 122, 125-7, 130, 133, 150a & b, 153b, 155, 168; Robert Haley, 16, 156a & b; Peter Jackson, 21; Reference Library, Blackpool, 6, 10, 29, 30, 33, 42-5, 52, 59, 66, 70, 72, 80-3, 91, 92, 98, 100, 101, 103, 107-9, 111, 140, 146, 148, 149, 153a; St John's parish church, 20; Barry Shaw, 61; W. John Smith, F.S.A., dustjacket, frontispiece, 4, 5, 8, 9, 14, 15, 17-19, 23-8, 32, 36-9, 41a & b, 46, 48-50, 55-7, 62, 63, 71, 73-5, 85, 89, 93, 95, 161; Studio D, 53, 84, 87, 99, 115-16, 118, 120, 123, 124, 128, 131, 132, 137, 164.

# Introduction

Blackpool began as part of the sparsely populated coastal area of the township of Layton with Warbreck. Layton, like many other Fylde villages, is mentioned in the Domesday Survey. In the Middle Ages, it appears to have been of greater relative importance, having been the first village in the Fylde to be granted a market in 1257. The Butlers, the Barons of Warrington, had a manor house there. The hamlet of Warbreck, first mentioned in the 12th century, stood near the water tower on Beryl Hill and its name suggests that it was originally a Scandinavian settlement. Although there are several examples in the Fylde of this ancient linking of Anglo-Saxon and Norse settlements, the reasons for it are obscure.

The medieval village of Great Layton stretched along Layton Road between Newton Drive and a little beyond Caunce Street. Nineteenth-century maps show empty burghage plots along the lane, indicating its decline. Its market cross and stocks, which had stood near Lawrence Bailey's old farmhouse on Layton Road, were only remembered by the oldest inhabitants when Thornber wrote Blackpool's history in 1837 and its Tudor hall had been replaced by a farmhouse about 1770.

From the south end of the village street, Dykes Lane ran to the west along the line of our modern Newton Drive until it joined a track known as Layton Rakes,[1] now Church Street. It passed a small community, which took its name from the track, a little beyond Devonshire Square. From there it ascended Rakes Hill before dropping down towards the sea shore at Lane's End. The word 'Rake' is Scandinavian in origin and denotes a path, especially one with a gradient and used for cattle. It seems likely that Layton Rakes was originally used to take cattle to pasture on Rakes Hill and beyond. Later the seaward end was to form the main hub of Blackpool's development.

From the vicinity of Layton Hall, another track led south-westerly, running a little south of Hornby Road and then on to Chapel Street and the sea. It was in this area that Lower Blackpool, as it was known in the 19th century, developed. Alan Stott[2] has identified the nucleus of this settlement as a dwelling known as the Pulhouse by the close of the 15th century. It stood near the junction of Kent Road and Princess Street and was marked 'Ruin' on the first O.S. map. At that time it was owned by Cockersand Abbey, which had obtained it from Amuria, the daughter of Richard, founder of Lytham Priory. The Pulhouse's land had been part of the estate of her great-great-grandfather, Raganald, a local thane at the time of the Norman Conquest. He was undoubtedly a descendant of 10th-century Viking settlers.

The Pulhouse is shown, along with two other houses, as 'The Pole Howses alias the North Howses' on a map prepared for a court case of 1532. The others were probably Warbreck's, an old longhouse on the south side of Chapel Street, which survived beyond the middle of the 19th century, and Cooban's at the junction of Princess Street and Blundell Street. The court proceedings themselves, a boundary dispute between the Butlers of Layton and the Prior of Lytham, make no mention of Pool Houses. However, 'the Houndehill in Laton' is mentioned as being the northern extent of the Hawes, the coastal tract which stretched as far as Lytham. On the crude map of 1532, the Pool Houses are shown to the north of a wide stream called 'The Mylne pole' running from 'The Mear' and driving 'The Mylne' at 'Grett Marton' with tributaries draining 'Myggeland' and 'Stonysykpole'. Two hundred years later, Marton Mere was greatly reduced by the cutting and widening of the Main Dyke north-eastwards to the Wyre, into which it naturally drained. As a result, Marton's watermill became inoperable. However, the dark coloured stream still ran further to the west draining Marton Moss, where it was known as Spen Dyke. It reached the sea near Manchester Square, where it became known as Black Pool.

Other coastal communities existed to the north at least as far back as the 17th century. In addition to dwellings near the Lane's End there was Fumblers Hill, which comprised several cottages extending westwards towards the edge of the cliff. Those remaining were demolished in 1897 to create Cocker Square. The inhabitants of these isolated hamlets lived their lives practically unnoticed by the outside world and it is only their basic details that have come down to us in Bispham's parish registers and in the occasional surviving will. It is in the register for 1602 that 'blackpoole' is mentioned for the first time, when Ellen Cooban's baptism was recorded.

About 1680, Edward Tyldesley of Myerscough, son of the Royalist Sir Thomas Tyldesley, built Foxhall, giving the hamlet of Lower Blackpool its first building of any substance. After Edward's death in 1685, his son Thomas, the diarist, had the hall. He is reputed to have kept a fox kennelled there. However, Alan Stott has suggested that the house's name came from its land being called 'Foxholes', itself derived from 'fosse', meaning a ditch, and the Old English 'hol', a hollow. This ties in with the topography of this low-lying area with Spen Dyke nearby.

By the beginning of the 18th century, doctors were advocating the drinking of sea water as a cure-all and the adoption of this practice, along with the complementary activity of sea bathing, precipitated the development of seaside resorts in this country. The growth was slow at first, but a great fillip was provided in 1783 by the royal patronage of Brighton.

Scarborough is reputed to have been the first English resort (1730s), having been established as a spa in the previous century. It is not known when Blackpool first attracted bathers and sea water drinkers, but people with social pretensions have always been quick to copy others and it seems likely that the fashion would have soon crossed the Pennines, at least on a small scale. Some have wondered why people were attracted to such a remote and featureless coast, devoid of bays. But as well as having a fine beach and sand hills to the south, Blackpool had natural cliffs to the north which were the most southerly on the Lancashire coast.

Friends of the Tyldesleys could be regarded as Blackpool's first visitors, but their only activity on the beach was likely to have been riding, in addition to gambling on horse and foot races on the Hawes. In 1745, it is recorded that Elizabeth Byrom and her brother, Edward, spent a day riding on the sands at Blackpool and Lytham. In 1754, while staying overnight at Poulton, Bishop Pococke mentioned in his diary that 'at Blackpool, near the sea, are accommodations for people who come to bathe'. These people undoubtedly stayed at local inns and four Blackpool innkeepers, John Forshaw, Thomas Gaulter, John Hobson and Richard Hodkinson, are listed in the 1755 Recognizance Roll. However, Thornber mentions one, Edward Whiteside, as having the first habitation to be fitted up for the reception of company. This was at Fumblers Hill, which had the advantage of a supply of water from a spring.

When the sea bathing explosion came in the 1780s, Blackpool was sufficiently well established to take advantage of it. Also, as W. John Smith has pointed out, the disposal of Sir Alexander Rigby's estates earlier in the century had eventually resulted in independent freeholders who were able to develop their land as they wished in order to cater for the visitors.

It was in the 1780s that Blackpool finally emerged from the mists of obscurity when its hoteliers began to advertise in the *Manchester Mercury* and in June 1783 a stage coach service between Manchester and Blackpool was advertised. At long last, in 1789, a description of the little resort was published by William Hutton, a Birmingham businessman, following his visit the year before.

By this time, Blackpool comprised about fifty mainly thatched dwellings around some half-dozen hotels spread along the coast. Near its northern boundary at Warbreck Ginn (meaning 'a track down to the sea'), stood the *Gynn Inn*, then an accommodation house. It survived until 1921 on the site of the present roundabout. Travelling south along Warbreck (Dickson) Road, past Hill Farm (rear of *Pembroke Hotel*) and among the cottages of Fumblers Hill, *Bailey's Hotel* was reached. It had been built on a promontory *c.*1784 by Lawrence Bailey, a yeoman farmer of Layton, and developed into *Butlin's Metropole Hotel*. To the east of it was a large barn and to the south a bath house. *Forshaw's Hotel*, one of the first in the resort, was next. Part of it survived until 1876 when the present west façade of the *Clifton Hotel* was built.

In front of *Forshaw's* was an alcove from which commenced the parade, described by Hutton as 'a pretty grass walk on the verge of the sea bank, divided from the road with white rails ... perhaps six yards wide and two hundred long'. At the southern end was 'a vile pit'. Nearby was the *Lane Ends Hotel*, built by Thomas Lewtas about 1780 and also known as the *Centre House* (Lewis's site). Next was *Hull's*, later the *Royal Hotel*, demolished in 1935 for Woolworth's department store.

Few buildings were then encountered until Bonny's Lane (Chapel Street) was reached. There, close to the pinfold where the *Wellington Hotel* later stood, John Bonny had built a bathing house to supplement his wine and lodging house further up the lane (*King Edward VII Hotel* site). Finally, between the pinfold and the by then dilapidated Foxhall, was *Elston's Hotel* on a low promontory, its only protection from the sea being the high banks of shingle then on the shore. It was later extended to become the *York Hotel* and demolished *c.*1875.

Recently, the account book of one of Blackpool's six principal hotels, *Bonny's*, was discovered. It covers the years 1785-94 and gives an insight into the scale of the operation. Taking a typical year, 1791, from the 'Baithing Account', a total of 232 people stayed that season, made up of four in May, seven in June, 39 in July, 111 in August, 43 in September and 28 in October. At a daily charge of 2s. 4d. for adults, 1s. 6d. for children and 1s. 8d. for servants, of which there had been 190, 26 and 16 respectively, the takings for the year amounted to £360 17s. 1d. plus a further £71 2s. 9d. taken for wine. The average length of stay was 14 nights and the names indicate that 34 of the guests had stayed at *Bonny's* in previous years.

By contrast with the 1780s, Blackpool's development during the next three decades was unspectacular and almost imperceptible. However, it could be said to have grown from a hamlet to a village during this time. In 1817 the need to educate the resort's growing number of children was met by the erection of the National Schools on Rakes Hill, for which a former visitor, John Gisborne, had raised funds. Four years later, St John's church was built and Blackpool's inhabitants and visitors no longer had to travel the three miles to Bispham in order to worship. In 1825 a Nonconformist chapel was erected on Bonny's Lane, which thus became known as Chapel Street.

During the 1820s, Henry Banks of the *Lane Ends Hotel* began to develop the Lane Ends Estate, which comprised the land on the south side of Church Street as far east as

Rakes Hill. He laid out Bank Hey Street and a drain along it to the meadows south of Hound Hill, Similar developments took place around Market Street as Lytham Charities leased some of the land on the north side of Church Street which they had bought as an investment in 1754.

W. John Smith possesses a diary of William Thornber, the third incumbent of St John's church and Blackpool's first local historian, in which he wrote intermittently from 1859-61. On 27 June 1861, Thornber described Blackpool as he remembered it in 1827-8. His account is given below, edited slightly to make it more comprehensible.

'When I first came here, the principle families were Robert Dickson's of the *Head Hotel*, Cuthbert Nickson's, now Birch's *Clifton Arms*, Thomas Nickson's the *Albion*, built afterwards, Henry Bank's *Lane Ends* and Gaskell's, afterwards Fisher's then Simpson's [*Royal Hotel*]. Henry Bank's brother, Robert, had retired to live on Church Street and Toppings then kept a small grocery. John Cocker came about two years after, driven from Blackburn by a gambling debt and in bad health. He came to Blackpool poor and had to lie in bed until his trousers were washed.

'Inns increased quickly. On Chapel Street, William Bonny, yeoman, lived at the old house [*Bonny's i' th' Fields*]. On the south side of Chapel Street, Richard Warbreck was at his, a low one storey whitened building with a barn the house part to the east, the kitchen to the west, then a shippon and a down dub to it. It has mullion lights and much oak furniture within.

'I must not omit nearby Nelson's Row [Bethesda Road]. The builder was formerly the owner of them as well as of some land. He left a portion for a school at Blackpool. The house he occupied has a porch and there was once a cupboard dated 1717. I placed this in the vestry. It was once a better kind of dwelling—a yeoman's. Facing the north, here lived an old family, the Archers, related to the Bambers, Bonnys, Warbrecks and Beals of Cleveleys and Bispham. The old man, in a fit, walked off one morning and was heard of no more.

'South Shore did not exist except for one house built by Thomas Moore. Only one old house existed on South Beach [later the Golden Mile], opposite Warbreck's, the property of a Pearson which, as he died without relatives, was claimed with its fields by the Lord of the Manor, Peter Hesketh, who sold it for £650 to John Bonny.

'Hound Hill could boast of a very old house or two. One was taken by Weston and is now in parts. It is now in the possession of the Parrs. Mr. Banks was born in it. Near Foxhall there was a row or two but most of them have been washed down.

'The highway went in front of Hygiene Terrace [Lewis's Store site]. All but three of these houses have been built since then. Up Church Street stood those [cottages] between the Temple of Arts and the Four Lane Ends, including one in which old Peel [Sir Robert's father] lodged. Then there were a few white cottages made from stables. Nearly opposite, but more to the west was a bowling green [British Home Stores site].

'Church Street was a hollow shelving down to a deep wide open ditch. Opposite the school, the road was very wide but since enclosed. It was formerly moor. There was no street across it, only a foot road up to Market Street.

'Where the *Albion* now stands [north corner of Church Street and the Promenade], billiard tables were kept up steps by George Cooke, the postmaster, who had been a royalist banished from America. Then came two good cottages, one called Cambells [*sic*] at the corner of Dig Street [West Street] which was then an impassable route near the sea and crossed by a ship's beam. On the north side of Dig Street was a grocer's shop and a post office, then another cottage.

'Next was old *Forshaw's Hotel* (*Clifton Arms*), ornamented with a shoemaker's shed on the east and faced by the alcove on the beach. Further still was a garden, walled in with cobbles, a stackyard and an outhouse, an old hut occupied by a very ancient dame. I know this well as I administered to her when she was dying. I remember the vast chimney, the mill stone hearth, the cat locker and pantry, with its latch and hatch door. The cock loft groaned with articles of all sorts.

'Opposite this hut was the new baths, erected by Dr. Swarbreck of Poulton and Henry Banks, which approached the shore by Peter's Slade. Here bricks were made to build the church. On the same side stood *Bailey's Hotel* and, in its yard, old Watt Bamber's cottage. Fumbler's pump was in use on the Hill where there was a row of buildings, at the end of which was Greenwood's, a neat little domicile, now a beer house. At right angles facing the sea, were three thatched dwellings open to a small green, now enclosed.

'John Hornby Esq. resided at Rakes Hall in summer. I was on good terms with him. General Yates, then Colonel, came over at times to Mount Pleasant [Fumblers Hill], which afterwards I was the means of purchasing but rogued out of my share.—Oh, brotherly love [an allusion to John Cocker, his brother-in-law].

'At Rakes Hill stood a smithy and house, and nearly opposite, another with a stable. At the Rakes was a row facing west and, facing south, two more. One was occupied by an old woman of 88 called Whalley and another, detached with an outhouse, by Blue Butcher. The verbena grew in the garden cop. I have since found it.'

In 1837, Dr. John Cocker, the father of Blackpool's first mayor, William H. Cocker, erected the Victoria Promenade on Green Walk, which developed into Victoria Street. The building, later known as the Crystal Palace, comprised an assembly room with folding windows opening onto a balcony. Below were seven shops. It can be regarded as the resort's first purpose-built public place of entertainment, although it seems to have provided little that was not already available at the leading hotels and in news and billiard rooms. Much of the building survives as the Majestic Restaurant at the northern corner of Bank Hey Street.

The year 1837 also saw the completion of West Hey, a large house erected by the Manchester banker, Sir Benjamin Heywood, as a summer residence. Standing on what was to become the site of the Tower, it was the grandest of many residences put up in Blackpool by wealthy businessmen during the 19th century.

As already mentioned, it had been the sale of parts of the manorial estate to small land owners that had enabled Blackpool to develop in the way it had. But it was to be the actions of the local gentry in the 1840s that would set Blackpool on course to become the country's leading resort by the end of the century.

In July 1840 a railway opened connecting Preston with the new port and town of Fleetwood, then being built by Sir Peter Hesketh Fleetwood, the Squire of Rossall. The line, which had a station at Poulton, immediately facilitated travel to Blackpool, the last four miles of the journey being served by coaches from its hotels. In 1842, Hesketh Fleetwood, by then in financial difficulty, sold the manorial rights of Layton to Thomas Clifton, the Squire of Lytham. Clifton, who already owned the Layton Hall Estate, bought part of the Forshaw Estate and laid out Talbot Road, Clifton Street and Abingdon Street. On 29 April 1846 a branch line from Poulton to Talbot Road station was opened. As cheap excursions had been introduced a few years before, all classes could now reach Blackpool easily and ever increasing numbers of visitors began to flow in.

In 1844, the first St John's Market had been erected on the site of the present municipal buildings, utilising Layton's 13th-century grant of a market. It bore the Clifton coat of arms, which can still be seen in the present St John's Market. Thereafter, Blackpool was no longer dependent on Poulton for its produce.

By 1851, Blackpool had grown large enough to require a body to run its affairs. This was arranged under the Public Health Act of 1848 by setting up the Local Board of Health for Layton with Warbreck. A small town hall was soon built for it on Market Street. In 1854, the Local Board was able to provide gas lighting and, in 1856, a new asphalt promenade was laid out. But it was left to the Fylde Waterworks Company to supply running water, though this was as late as 1864.

Although it now possessed some utilities, Blackpool still lacked entertainment for its visitors. The North Pier, opened in 1863, was certainly an added attraction to visitors who were fascinated by the sea in all its moods, but at that time the pier only had shelters on it. It was in 1868, the year its second pier opened, that the resort got its first purpose-built theatre, the Theatre Royal, later the Tivoli cinema, in Talbot Square. The 1860s also saw the development of the Claremont Park estate northwards to the Gynn and the decade ended with a new promenade and sea defences nearing completion. Of equal significance were the many churches erected in the town at this time.

In the 1870s there was an explosive increase in the resort's attractions. Raikes Hall's pleasure gardens opened in 1872; facilities and buildings were added to it almost yearly. In 1875, W.H. Cocker opened his aquarium and menagerie on Central Beach to the public. The Winter Gardens Company, formed the same year, operated a roller-skating rink from 1876 and the main pavilion opened in 1878. The previous year had seen the opening of the Borough Theatre, North Pier's Indian Theatre and the Prince of Wales Theatre on the Promenade,

In 1876, Blackpool was granted a charter of incorporation and elected W.H. Cocker as its first mayor. In 1879, the Corporation pioneered electric street lighting by installing Siemens arc lamps along the Promenade. Just as innovative was the introduction, six years later, of an electric tramway, running between Cocker Street and Station Road.

The opening of the Opera House alongside the Winter Gardens on 10 June 1889 may be seen as the start of the second wave of Blackpool's entertainment boom. Soon the Grand Circus was operating, developing into the Grand Theatre by 1894. In 1893, the Victoria Pier, along with its Grand Pavilion, was completed at South Shore. With the Tower in 1894 came its circus, roof garden and first ballroom. The Winter Gardens Company responded in 1896 with the Empress Ballroom, Indian Lounge and Italian Gardens. As a counter attraction to the Tower itself, the Big Wheel was built. In Church Street a large theatre called the Empire was built in 1895. After changing hands in 1900 it became the Hippodrome.

In 1899, the lavish Alhambra opened alongside the Tower on the site of the Prince of Wales Theatre and Baths, built only 20 years before. The new building housed a theatre, ballroom and a circus even more luxurious than the Tower's. The same year saw the completion of the present Tower Ballroom. Blackpool entered the 20th century unrivalled as a resort in its wealth of entertainments.

Three manifestations of popular entertainment in Blackpool in the 20th century, the Pleasure Beach, the Golden Mile and the cinema, had their roots in the 1890s. During that decade, a small fairground had developed by the sand-hills at South Shore. From 1904, when Maxim's 'Flying Machine' began running, it began to develop in earnest with new rides, many brought from America, being added yearly. It has been developing ever since as Blackpool Pleasure Beach.

On 2 March 1897, following a petition against the nuisance of touting presented by over 800 company house keepers, the Council decided to 'let ventriloquists, niggers, Punch and Judy, boatmen, donkeys, camels, ice cream, ginger beer, Blackpool rock, sweets in baskets and oyster sellers return to the Sands, but not the following: Drapers, dealers in fancy goods of all sorts, quack doctors, phrenologists, palmists, cheap Jacks, and all stands and stalls'. The banned group merely moved to the gardens of the houses along South Beach. These gardens soon became forecourts and gradually the Golden Mile was formed.

The first demonstrations of moving pictures in Blackpool had taken place in 1897 at the Cosy Café in Bank Hey Street and in the Tower's ballroom. An early newsreel had shown the wreck of Nelson's old ship, the *Foudroyant*, near North Pier that year. From March 1907, a full length programme of films was being shown at the Colosseum, Tyldesley Road, and in 1909 the town's first purpose-built cinema, the Royal Pavilion, opened opposite. By the start of the First World War, Blackpool had seven cinemas and at least five theatres and other buildings in use as cinemas.

1899 had seen the completion of a sea wall as far as the Gynn, involving the building of lower and middle walks. At the same time, the toll levied for travel through Claremont Park was abolished. In 1902, work began on a new sea wall and the widening of the Promenade by 100ft., starting at South Shore and ending just beyond North Pier in 1905. In 1912 the completion of Princess Parade connected the two previous schemes.

It was in the first years of the century that the tramway's potential was fully realised. It was taken off the roadway on to the new Promenade and new lines were laid inland to Layton, Marton and along Central Drive. There were also improvements to Blackpool's rail connections. Both North and Central stations had been rebuilt by 1900 and in 1903 a direct line from Kirkham to South Shore and Central stations was inaugurated. In 1902 Preston New Road was completed. With subsequent improvements along the route, it greatly eased travel by road from Preston and beyond.

Blackpool was always eager to encourage new developments, if only for their novelty value. In October 1904 it staged its first motor speed trials along the new Promenade, where the British record of 84 m.p.h. was equalled. Similarly, it embraced aviation by staging practically the first meeting in the country at Squires Gate in 1909. The famous Illuminations started on a small scale in 1912, but had to be suspended in 1914. They were re-introduced in 1925.

In 1914, the sea wall was extended from the Gynn to the Bispham boundary and sunken gardens were laid out, opening in 1915. In April 1918, Bispham cum Norbreck was absorbed into the County Borough of Blackpool and work continued on the construction of sea defences further northwards. From 1921, Devonshire Road was built between Talbot Road and Bispham.

Throughout the 1920s, large municipal schemes were undertaken, their hallmark being the neo-classical styling of their features. Colonnades were constructed along the Middle Walk at North Shore. North of the Gynn, the cliffs were faced in concrete to form a rockery. At South Shore, large open air baths opened at the beginning of Carnival Week in 1923. From there to Squires Gate, a new promenade was built with its sea wall 400ft. westward of the old beach. To the east of the town, Stanley Park, including a golf course and lake, was laid out at a cost of £250,000; part of it opened in 1925. Further east, on a site recommended by Sir Alan Cobham, a municipal aerodrome was built and in use from 1929.

The only large private scheme at this time was the modernisation of the Winter Gardens after they had been taken over by the Tower Company in 1928. The Big Wheel was dismantled and the Olympia exhibition hall was erected where it had stood. In the upper part of the Victoria Street entrance, the Spanish Hall was created, along with the adjacent Baronial hall, Renaissance Restaurant and Galleon Bar. The complex opened in May 1931.

Despite the depression, the 1930s are remembered as Blackpool's heyday. It received enormous publicity from the films and radio broadcasts of popular entertainers who performed there. In a decade that was eager to shake off the Victorian ethos, Blackpool strove to be modern. The first of Blackpool's familiar streamlined trams was introduced in 1933 and soon many cream-tiled buildings were to be seen about the town. In 1936, Blackpool was described as 'the streamlined resort'.

The last half of the 1930s saw an unprecedented spate of building. Such buildings as St John's Market, Talbot Road bus station, the Technical College, Harrowside Solarium, the Casino, Opera House, Savoy Café, North Pier's theatre, Woolworth's, the Co-op Emporium, Derby Baths and the Odeon cinema were erected and, in addition, many public houses were built. An ambitious scheme to move Central station back to Chapel Street and create a new civic centre had to be abandoned because of the Second World War. Similarly, the large shopping arcade intended to replace the property between Market Street and Corporation Street, demolished in 1939, was never built.

During the war, Blackpool was used as a base for training RAF personnel on a large scale and many of its buildings were commandeered. Because of the large military presence in the town, the entertainment industry was encouraged to keep going during the war. Therefore, Blackpool, unlike many resorts in the more vulnerable South, was quickly able to re-establish its position after the war had ended.

In the late 1940s and throughout the 1950s, Blackpool provided the same diversions as it had done before the war. It boasted as many as 15 live shows during the season and was able to attract the top British artistes as well as internationally famous stars. From the 1960s onwards, changing tastes and expectations brought about by television, consumerism, jet travel and other factors began to bite. Unlike many resorts, Blackpool was able to respond. As the number of variety shows declined, nightclub-style entertainment, bingo and amusement arcades proliferated.

In 1967, the Tower Company was taken over by EMI, and Trust House Forte by then controlled the piers. Much of the Golden Mile was replaced with box-like arcades; everything was given the bland sixties look. As a backdrop, in the early 1970s Bonny's Estate was redeveloped with a slab concrete police station, courts and multi-storey car park. Then the vast Coral Island amusement centre was built on the site of Central station and the *New Inn*.

The opening of the M55 motorway link to Blackpool in 1975 has resulted in more day visitors, thereby affecting hotels and guest houses. Despite pedestrianisation and the redevelopment of the Victoria Street area to create the Hounds Hill Shopping Centre in 1980, there is a feeling that Blackpool is no longer a place for quality shopping. Since the loss of several department stores, the M55 often takes the town's residents on shopping expeditions to Preston and Bolton.

Notwithstanding, Blackpool still continues to attract outside investment and visitors alike. The Golden Mile and the piers have now recovered from sixties minimalism and are brighter and more colourful than ever before. In 1994 replicas of Edwardian shelters and a bandstand have greatly enhanced the appearance of Central Promenade and work is in progress on a sewage scheme to alleviate pollution of the sea and beach—the very two elements that brought Blackpool into being.

[1] In his diary for 1861, William Thornber states that the spelling was changed to 'Raikes' by the owner of Raikes Hall, presumably to avoid unfortunate connotations.

[2] In a paper, 'Blackpool's Mediaeval Foundation', read to the Blackpool & Fylde Historical Society, 30 November 1988.

1. Foxhall, Blackpool's first substantial building, was erected as a coastal retreat by Edward Tyldesley of Myerscough, *c.*1680. His father was the Royalist, Sir Thomas Tyldesley, killed at the battle of Wigan Lane in 1651. Reproduced here is the bookplate of Edward's son, Thomas. Interestingly, only Foxhall is mentioned, suggesting that it, not Myerscough Lodge, was then his main residence.

2. This 1865 photograph shows uniquely the old whitewashed farm buildings of Foxhall behind the *Foxhall Hotel*. When the hotel was demolished in December 1990, its south bay was found to have been part of a cobbled house running west-east. To the right is what remained of a lofty cobbled wall which once surrounded the old hall. It collapsed in a hurricane on 29 January 1877.

3.  Blackpool was included in the manor of Layton. This house, Layton Hall Farm, replaced the Tudor manor house *c*.1770, but was itself demolished in 1927. A solitary pear tree survives on Collingwood Avenue. The gateposts of the earlier hall were re-erected inside Stanley Park. However, subsequent rebuilding at the south of the park has left only the tops recognisable.

4.  In 1837, Thornber wrote that Layton's village was composed of very mean houses. This is borne out by the photograph, *c*.1912, showing labourers' cottages on Layton Lane near Hollywood Avenue. Although picturesque, the snow scene has an air of poverty. Between the wars, a sea of semis spread beyond Layton; Blackpool had engulfed the village that had spawned it.

5.  Humble cottages of this kind were once common in the Blackpool area, but few now remain. This is Pepper Hill, which stood opposite the *No.4 Hotel* on Layton Lane until *c*.1900. Its cobbled garden wall remains, although its height has since been doubled.

6.  Before 1821, this small whitewashed church at Bispham would have been familiar to Blackpool's inhabitants as their place of worship. The graves of many of them can still be seen in the churchyard. It was pulled down in June 1883, being superseded by Bispham's present parish church. Seated on a tombstone are the dialect poets, Samuel Laycock and Edwin Waugh.

7. Despite Blackpool's popularity from the late 18th century this is the earliest authentic representation from Peter Whittle's *Marina*, published in 1831. It shows the sea front from *Nickson's Hotel*, later the *Clifton Arms*, to the *Lane Ends Hotel*. Campbell's Cottage on Dig (West) Street, with its gable end facing the sea, stood on the site of Roberts Oyster Rooms.

8. *Bonny's i' th' Fields* was one of Blackpool's first lodging houses. Formerly known as *Old Margery's* after its owner, Margery Hobson, John Bonny ran it from 1785 and by 1787 had built the taller extension to the west. It was demolished in 1902 and the *King Edward VII Hotel* was built on its site at the end of Chapel Street.

9. Rakes Smithy was reputedly Blackpool's oldest building, estimated to be 300 years old. Before its demolition in 1989 it had been a bedding shop on Church Street opposite Park Road. In the early 19th century John Carter, the father of Esau, Blackpool's postmaster, was blacksmith there. It is seen here when Michael Parker had it.

10. Blackpool's first Independent chapel, which opened 6 July 1825, is seen here from the corner of Kent and Bethesda Roads. After Victoria Street Congregational church was opened in 1849, it was used periodically by the Methodists until again becoming a Congregational chapel in 1875 and later a school. A new Bethesda church, opened on 5 June 1901, replaced the building.

*Albert Terrace, Blackpool.*
*From the Sea.*

11.   An 1852 engraving showing *Bailey's Hotel* and Albert Terrace, completed in 1848. Nearby, access to the beach is provided by Peter's Slade. The small building on the right is Dr. Baker's house in Talbot Square on the site of *Yates's Wine Lodge*.

*Blackpool*

12.   Central Beach, *c*.1852, showing the flagstaff at the end of Victoria Street, the *Beach Hotel* and Sir Benjamin Heywood's house, West Hey, on the site of the Tower. The *Royal Hotel* is in the middle and to the right is Queen's Terrace. This engraving would have been sold in publisher George White's premises round the corner in Adelaide Place.

13.   In the 1850s, South Shore was a small town, still quite separate from Blackpool. The first houses had been erected there in 1819 by Thomas Moore, the miller of Great Marton. In the engraving, a marine tower can be discerned at the end of Waterloo Road.

*South Shore, Blackpool.*
*From the Sea*

14. Blackpool Pier, later North Pier, was a simple structure when opened on 21 May 1863. It was considered a great novelty at a time when visitors were content just to gaze at the sea; the resort had few other attractions. Now people were able to walk over the waves yet remain safe and dry.

15. Photographed from within the garden of Burnley House at Fumblers Hill (*see* plate 25), Cliff Cottage is seen here shortly before its demolition *c*.1865 to allow the promenade to be extended northwards to the Gynn. It faced south with its barn close to the cliff edge.

16. This unique 1864 photograph shows the wooden 'Bridge of Peace' built in 1856 with a 90° turn across the Lane Ends Ginn. It lasted until 1870, when a new promenade and sea defences replaced the cobble rammed clay embankment visible in the picture. Behind, the *Lane Ends Hotel* is being rebuilt while its bath house of 1836 remains alongside.

17.   An 1865 beach scene near the Lane Ends Ginn, with the re-erected *Lane Ends Hotel* on the right and North Pier in the distance. The old *Clifton Arms Hotel* can be seen beyond the bridge.

18.   Looking along the parade from the top of the Lane Ends Ginn *c.*1866, showing Hygiene Terrace on the left. The *Beach Hotel* and the darker West Hey House can both be seen where the Tower now stands. Beyond, well in front of the building line, is the *Royal Hotel*, dating from the 18th century.

19.  *Bailey's Hotel* was built on a promontory by Lawrence Bailey, a Layton farmer, *c.*1784. Across the road, the barn of the hotel's farm survives in this photograph taken *c.*1870. By the late 1890s, the hotel had developed into the *Metropole*, currently run by Butlin's.

20.  The first St John's church, consecrated on 6 July 1821, is seen here from the corner of Cedar Street. The church had been re-roofed in 1862 and a new larger tower had been erected in 1866. The last service there took place on 11 March 1877. Shortly afterwards the entire building was pulled down and the present church erected.

21.   The *Wellington Hotel*, seen here *c*.1866, was built in 1851 by Robert Bickerstaffe on the site of Lower Blackpool's pinfold near Chapel Street. The boats testify to the Bickerstaffes' involvement with the sea. Robert's nephew, Bob, was the famous coxswain of the lifeboat. Robert's son, John, took over as manager of the *Wellington* before becoming chairman of the Tower Company.

22.  This section of a panoramic photograph, taken in 1865 to promote South (now Central) Pier, shows cottages facing Foxhall Road, south of the *Wellington Hotel*. There were no coastal road or sea defences in this area. On the left, houses on the east side of Foxhall Road are being built. To the right are Wylie's cottages.

23.  Wylie's *South Pier Hotel* stood well forward of the building line on South Beach by Chapel Street. It originated in the 18th century as John Bonny's bath house. Later Jonathan Wylie opened it as the *Sea Beach Hotel*, changing its name when South (now Central) Pier was built. Following demolition, *c.*1904, its licence was transferred to the *King Edward VII Hotel*.

24. Nile and Lion cottages stood on Chapel Street, just behind Wylie's *South Pier Hotel*. Once popularly regarded as being fishermen's cottages, they were demolished about 1904 to make way for 'Fairyland'.

25. These cottages of the old community of Fumbler's Hill lasted until 1897 on what is now the car park in Cocker Square. In the centre is Burnley House with James Crabtree's post office and grocery store. On Cocker Street to the right are the swimming baths built by Chris Johnson *c.*1871 and refitted by Jonathan Reed, re-opening in July 1873.

26a & b. The Union Baptist chapel opened in Abingdon Street on 29 March 1861. A new Baptist church was opened in Springfield Road on 1 March 1905. The chapel had been sold to the Government on 12 October 1903 for the site of a new general post office, but it was not demolished until as late as 1907, its Sunday school having been used as a branch post office.

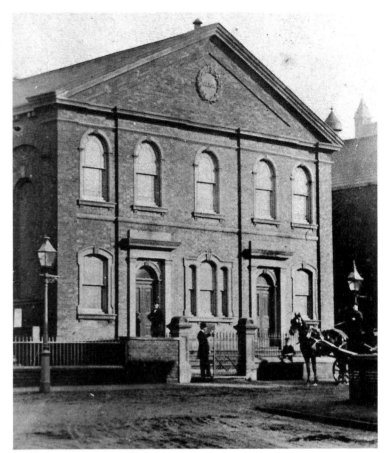

27.  *(above left)* These Regency-style houses at the south end of Queen's Terrace, on the sea front, date from the early 19th century. The *Palatine Hotel* was built on their site in the late 1870s.

28.  *(below left)* The entrance to the old Hounds Hill station, later Central station, *c.*1880 showing the old *New Inn and Central Hotel*, rebuilt in 1896. Next to it are the backs of cottages on South Beach which overlooked Brewer's Meadow before the Blackpool and Lytham Railway was built in 1862.

29. *(above)* The south side of Queen Street *c*.1870 with Sacred Heart church's tower behind. The end terrace house to the right, where The Strand was put through, later belonged to Dr. Thomas McNaughton, mayor in 1880 and 1885. Later Queen Street became the most select shopping area in Blackpool but has since declined, although there are plans to revitalise it.

30. *(right)* Talbot Road was built by Thomas Clifton of Lytham Hall on land he had acquired from the Forshaw estate on 2 February 1843. It is shown *c*.1875 looking towards the sea from Dickson Road, then called Station Road as far as Queen Street. On the right is Robert Nickson's *Station Hotel* which was taken over by his son, Fred, in the 1880s.

31.    The *Clifton Arms* in the early 1870s. The four-storey wing at the rear was completed in 1866. In 1876 the hotel's older buildings along the promenade were replaced. In the foreground are ornate cast-iron gates added to North Pier in 1869.

32.   The foundation stone of the Sacred Heart, Talbot Road, Blackpool's first Roman Catholic church, was laid 30 May 1856 and it was opened 8 December 1857. It had been designed by Edward W. Pugin, the son of the famous Augustus W.N. Pugin. On the right is the 1859 presbytery, demolished when the large octagonal extension to the church was added in 1894.

33.   The Central Methodist chapel, at the corner of Adelaide Street and Bank Hey Street, was opened on 4 July 1862, replacing Blackpool's first Methodist chapel erected a little to the east in 1835. The tower was only added in the 1890s when the building was re-faced in terracotta. The building was demolished 1972-3. The present church is above shops on the site.

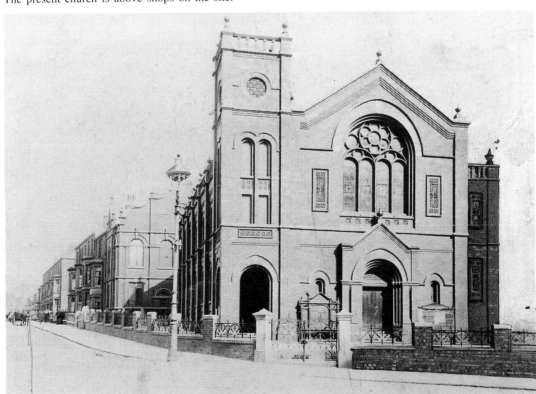

34. *The Fleece Hotel*, Market Street, *c*.1895, when Thomas Astley was the licensee. Built by Richard Braithwaite, it was known as the *Golden Fleece* by 1848 and as the *Fleece Inn* by 1856. The present hotel, designed by Halstead Best, was erected in 1938. Behind in West Street is a glimpse of 18th-century property once known as Dobson's Row.

35.  North Shore *c*.1897, showing the newly built sea defences as far north as the Gynn. Above them, work continues on the Middle Promenade. In the distance, *Uncle Tom's Cabin* can be discerned on the Bispham cliffs.

36.   The view from North Pier towards North Shore in the 1880s. The angle of the bathing vans indicates a greater slope to the liberally pebbled beach on which traders have set up trestle tables. An iron walkway surmounts the sloping sea defences completed in 1870 around *Bailey's Hotel*.

37.  In 1863 the Blackpool Land, Building and Hotel Company
purchased the land between Fumblers Hill and the Gynn to build
Claremont Park. To keep the estate exclusive, toll gates were
placed at both ends of Queens Drive. The photograph, *c*.1890,
shows Imperial Terrace, formerly Adelaide Terrace, with the
*Imperial Hotel* of 1867 beyond. All these smart houses are now
hotels with obligatory sun lounges.

38. *Uncle Tom's Cabin* began as a refreshment stall on the Bispham cliffs in the 1850s. By the time of this 1882 photograph, it had a full licence and a music hall. Above the dance hall, the effigies of characters from the famous novel have been joined by three real-life characters from the establishment beneath. The more westerly buildings were later undermined by coastal erosion and those remaining were demolished in January 1908.

39. The once solitary *Foxhall Hotel* found itself dwarfed by large lodging houses as South Parade was built to the north and Tyldesley Terrace to the south in 1880. Here, looking towards South (now Central) Pier *c*.1890, a single conduit system tramtrack runs along the cobbled promenade.

40. *(left)* The imposing entrance to Raikes Hall Gardens is seen here from the corner of Park Road, with houses on Raikes Road, now Church Street, on the left. The gardens had opened to the public in 1872 and were bounded by Raikes Road, Whitegate Drive, Hornby Road and Raikes Parade. The gates, which stood at the eastern end of the present grassed area in front of the Salvation Army Citadel, were taken down in 1904.

41a & b. *(below left and right)* During its 30-year life, many buildings and features were added to Raikes Hall Gardens to entice visitors away from the seaside attractions. Behind the fountain is a large aviary; behind that is the monkey house opened in 1887. To the right is the roller-skating rink which was surrounded by a conservatory.

42.   Looking up Church Street from the entrance to the Winter Gardens towards Cedar Villas in 1879. Mount Tabor Cottage displays the posters of Henry Hutchinson, who appears to have employed multi-media advertising techniques. The gable end remained after the cottage was demolished in 1894. It was May 1898 before the Winter Gardens Company was persuaded to remove this obstacle to the footpath.

43.   This photograph, looking up Market Street in 1879, was taken outside Richard Wade's grocery at the corner of Church Street and Bank Hey Street. The property on the left, dated 1874, still exists. However, George Bolton's drapery shop, opposite, in property dated 1868, was cleared away in 1939 to allow the widening of Market Street. Previously, Rose Cottage had stood there.

44.   Market Street is seen here in 1879, looking south from Euston Street, which once ran east-west through the British Home Stores site. On the left is the door of the *Castle Inn*, demolished with other property in 1939, not just for re-development but also to allow road widening. Opposite, with the sun-blind down, is Thomas Masheter's butcher's, established in 1851.

45.   The view along Church Street in 1879 from the vicinity of Marks and Spencer. The gable end of Ellen Banks' cottage is on the left. She was the daughter of Lawrence Bailey and had married Robert Banks of the *Lane Ends Hotel*. The poster advertises the roller-skating rink at the Winter Gardens.

46. In July 1867, Sir Benjamin Heywood's former house, West Hey, was opened as The Prince of Wales Arcade by Thomas Love, wings being added to the building. The premises were later acquired by W.H. Cocker who built an aquarium in the south wing which he opened to the public on 17 May 1875. It is seen here *c*.1890, shortly before it was acquired as the site of the Tower.

47. On the beach towards South Shore an elephant from the Blackpool Aquarium, Aviary and Menagerie is being used to advertise the establishment. In the background is a partially completed St Chad's Terrace, which bears the date 1891.

48. The imposing Winter Gardens Pavilion of 1878. Only the top of the pavilion can now be seen above the Olympia buildings. On the left is the Victoria Street entrance hall. Bank Hey House, sold by W.H. Cocker, had been incorporated into the building, its position being that of the amusement arcade off the Floral Hall.

49. The theatre of the Winter Gardens Pavilion could be opened to the surrounding 'Horseshoe' perambulatory area. In 1989 the stage area was removed and the floor raised to the level of the Horseshoe.

50.   A crowded Central Beach about four years before the Tower transformed the skyline. The *Palatine Hotel*, erected in the late 1870s, predominates. On the right, where 'Coral Island' now stands, is the old *New Inn*, rebuilt in 1896. Small gas lamps line the Promenade, while the electric arc lamps of 1879 can be seen on high posts.

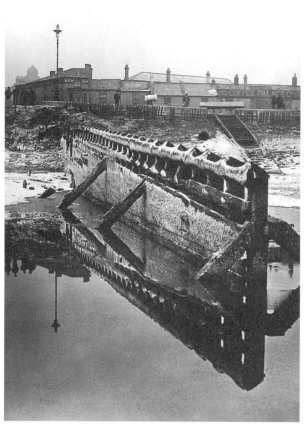

51. One of several unsightly groynes placed across the beach in the 1880s, photographed during the winter of 1894-5. The roof of Central station can be seen behind the old cottages next to the *New Inn*.

52. Blackpool's second pier was opened on 30 May 1868. It was known as South Pier until the Victoria Pier was built at South Shore in 1893, when it became Central Pier. It is seen here in the 1880s when it seemed every available surface was used for advertising.

53.   Regarded as 'the people's pier', Central Pier, seen here *c.*1905, was renowned for open-air dancing which continued until 1964. The dancing was often spontaneous and could take place almost anywhere on the pier. In contrast to the elegance displayed on North Pier (*see* plate 56), some of the dancers are wearing shawls.

54.   The Prince of Wales Theatre, with a market beneath, opened 20 August 1877 on the former site of Hygiene Terrace, a row of genteel houses dating from the 1830s. The adjoining swimming baths, renowned for aquatic shows, opened in 1881. Photographed in 1894 when the Tower's first ballroom was under construction to the south, its site was cleared three years later for the Alhambra.

55.   North Pier, photographed from the new Town Hall in 1900. The pier had been widened from 28ft. to 48ft. in 1895 and new Indian-style shelters placed along it. The kiosks at the landward end lasted until 1903, when an eastern-style pavilion was built.

56. *(below)* The pier-head of North Pier was enlarged in 1875 by the addition of two wings. A bandstand was erected on the south wing, seen here *c.*1890, with a seated audience, many with parasols to preserve their pale complexions. On the north wing stood the Indian Pavilion, which forms the background.

57. *(right)* The popularity of excursions by paddle steamer in late Victorian times can be judged by this scene at North Pier's double jetty. Trips could be taken to Llandudno, Liverpool, Southport, Morecambe, Barrow and Douglas.

58. *(below right)* On 9 October 1892, the 150ft. Norwegian barque, *Sirene*, ran aground in a storm, at the same time smashing into North Pier and demolishing part of the decking and four kiosks. The photograph shows clearly the sloping sea wall of 1870 and the promenade supported at this point on iron stanchions.

59. The Victoria Schools, Tyldesley Road, opened in 1888. In 1915 the school was extensively altered and a storey added. Because of the shortage of space, the playground was placed on the flat roof. The building was purchased by the Government in the 1920s and used by the Department of Employment until 1993. It was demolished in 1994.

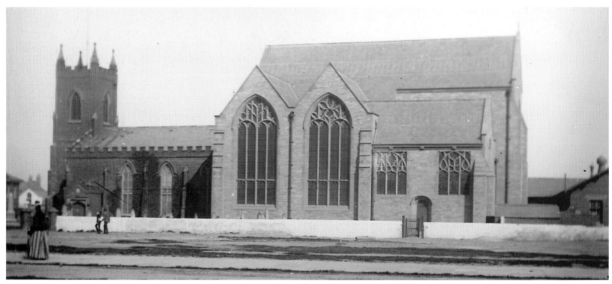

60. South Shore's original church of 1836 is seen on the left of this view from Station Road. Attached to it is part of the new church, consecrated on 23 September 1889. The old church was demolished in 1894 to allow the completion of the west end of Holy Trinity, opened 27 November 1895. Some of the cobbled churchyard wall still survives.

61. This building at the corner of Coronation Street and Carter Street opened 5 December 1892 as Blackpool's main post office, replacing adjacent premises at the corner of Church Street. It was superseded by the GPO on Abingdon Street in 1910 and later became part of Marks and Spencer's store until it was redeveloped in the late 1970s.

62. Abingdon Street from Talbot Road, *c.*1895, with the Church Street entrance and cupola of the Winter Gardens in the background. Halfway down the street on the left, behind a gas lamp, is the former police station (1862) to which an extra storey has been added. Part of the building survives in Abingdon Street Market's frontage.

63. The hospital on Whitegate Drive was opened in August 1894. After the addition of wings which were opened on 7 August 1897, it was named the Victoria hospital. On 29 September 1936, patients were transferred to the new Victoria hospital at Whinney Heys. The old building remains as a health centre.

64. The foundation stone of Blackpool Tower was laid on 25 September 1891 and its foundations were put in during the winter. Construction of the Tower itself did not get under way until March 1892. Here the girders project skywards beyond 120ft. The south wing of the old aquarium building remained open and was eventually incorporated into the Tower building.

65. While the Tower has reached a height of 235ft., work continues at the first-floor level of the building around its base. The *Beach Hotel*, visible to the north of the site, survived until 10 October 1893.

66. During the summer of 1893, work on the Tower had reached 380ft., the level of the first viewing platform. It opened on Whit Monday, 14 May 1894, although the building at its base was unfinished.

67.   On 22 July 1897, about 11.15 p.m., a spectacular blaze caused by an electrical fault, occurred at the top of the Tower. Many people, some half dressed, turned out to see the fire which sent blazing debris into the streets below. It burnt itself out about 2 a.m. and, although the top was gutted, the structure, some of which had glowed red hot, was practically undamaged.

68. The Tower Menagerie had its origins in Dr. Cocker's Aquarium which opened on the site in 1875. The zoo was later immortalised by Stanley Holloway's monologue 'Albert and the Lion'. In June 1963 it was converted into 'the Ocean Room', a bar with live entertainment, but since 1992 the 'Dawn of Time' ride has occupied the space.

69. The Tower's sumptuous café restaurant was for many years the place to be seen, although after the last war it lost most of its elegance. It was destroyed in the fire which badly damaged the ballroom above it on 14 December 1956. The café was rebuilt as the Tower Lounge, a popular bar with entertainment.

70.   The Tower's roof gardens were once a place of tranquillity where one could sit and relax among exotic plants. At one end there was a stage for concerts and a puppet theatre. It is now 'Jungle Jim's', a children's adventure playground, where adults can experience the cacophony of a real jungle as the little monkeys clamber over rope bridges, nets and slides.

71. One of the first photographs taken from the top of the Tower in 1894. It shows open fields and farms to the north east of Pleasant Street and vacant plots on Dickson Road. To the left is the promontory on which *Bailey's Hotel* stood before Princess Parade was built. Below, the landward end of North Pier has already been repaired after the *Sirene* badly damaged it.

72.	(above) Looking south from the Tower c.1901. In the foreground are the boarding houses of South Beach, later the Golden Mile. Between them and Central station is Bonny's Estate, developed in the 1840s. An uninterrupted sea of houses stretches as far as Victoria Pier before sand hills are encountered at South Shore, which had been regarded as a separate town only 30 years before.

73.	(top right) The Great Wheel and the Winter Gardens, viewed from the upper balcony of the Tower building in 1896. The Hounds Hill Centre now occupies the foreground, to the left of which is the town's yard, the equivalent of the Council Depot. Nearby, on former Sefton Street, is the rear of the Victoria Street Congregational church, erected in 1849.

74.	(bottom right) This unusual photograph, taken from a rooftop in Adelaide Street, shows the newly completed Great Wheel between two of Blackpool's other great Victorian enterprises, the Tower and the Winter Gardens Pavilion. The Wheel, which opened 22 August 1896, stood 220ft. high.

75.   The *Gynn Inn*, once an 18th-century accommodation house, stood alone at the Warbreck Ginn, a track down to the sea, until the development of the Claremont Estate in 1860s, when the *Duke of Cambridge Hotel*, behind, was built. The latter, by contrast, had a full licence transferred to the present *Gynn Hotel* which replaced it in the late 1930s.

76.   The rustic charm of Bispham Village attracted visitors in the early 1900s and Blackpool might have thought to preserve it after taking over Bispham with Norbreck in 1918. This 1890s easterly view, from near the present roundabout, was transformed in the late 1950s by the building of a modern shopping centre. In the distance is the hipped roof of Ivy Cottage.

77. Bispham's cruck-built Ivy Cottage as it appeared in the 1890s with an attached barn. It became a tea room catering for visitors taking the stroll to the picturesque village from the tram stop on the cliffs. In the 1930s a painted plaster panel, dated 1686, was discovered inside. It was preserved when the building was demolished in 1958.

78. The hamlet of Norbreck *c*.1895. In the foreground is the marine residence, Norbreck Villa, with its gazebo. The arrival of the coastal tramway from Blackpool in 1898 precipitated the development of Norbreck and the villa became the *Norbreck Hydro*. Part of the villa, including its porch, can still be seen on Norbreck Road. Norbreck House in the distance occupied the site of the Travellers Club until *c*.1925.

79.  A young Allen Clarke, author of *Windmill Land*, stands on Pennystone Rock, *c*.1894. According to a local legend mentioned in 1789, an inn which sold ale for a penny a pot had once existed on the site. However, the rock probably fell on to the beach as the cliffs eroded, over 1,000 years ago. The only dwelling visible on the coast is Norbreck Villa.

80.  The west side of Bonny Street, behind the Golden Mile, taken from the vicinity of Chapel Street, *c*.1910. The old property in the foreground was cleared away shortly afterwards for the rear of the Trocadero building. On the right, in the distance, can be seen the *Brunswick Hotel*.

81. This procession along Church Street is probably a miners' demonstration which took place on 14 May 1898. On the left is the Liberal Club in a building which still bears the date 1879. The rear of the building contained the Clifton Livery Stables. On 1 March 1911 the premises opened as the Clifton Palace cinema which became the Tatler News Theatre from 1950 until 1954, when it became a furniture shop.

82. *(right)* 'Little Ben's' bowling green, at the corner of May Bell Avenue and Queen Street, formerly occupied the site of the Carnegie Library and Grundy Art Gallery, which were opened on 26 October 1911. Beyond are the backs of boarding houses erected in 1894 on Springfield Road. To the right is Christ Church vicarage, demolished *c*.1960 and now the site of a car park.

83. *(left)* Fire practice at the fire station in Albert Road. The brigade had moved into these premises in 1901, having previously occupied a small station in the town's yard, Sefton Street, from 1878. The fire brigade moved out of the town centre to a new station on Forest Gate in 1987.

84. *(below)* The Palace is seen here after 'talkie' equipment had been installed in June 1930. The building had opened in 1899 as the opulent Alhambra which comprised a circus, theatre, ballroom, restaurant and lounges. However, the enterprise was commercially unsuccessful, being wound up on 22 November 1902. The building was acquired by the Tower Company, and re-opened as the Palace on 4 July 1904.

85.  Talbot Square, 1894. East of the London and Midland Bank, with clock, is the row of shops which included the café of the Misses Jenkinson, now *Rumours Fun Pub*. Talbot Dining Rooms occupies the front of the 1868 Assembly Rooms. In May 1894, Peter Yates took over *Liston's Bar* to the rear as a wine bar and acquired the whole building in 1896.

86. *(above)* A deserted and decaying Raikes Hall Gardens, *c.*1902. The statuary and fountain stood in what is now Leamington Road, just in front of the *Raikes Hotel*. The trees lined a path which is now Liverpool Road, towards Church Street. A move to turn the gardens into a municipal park had been defeated and the land was largely built on in the 1920s.

87. *(top right)* The main entrance to the Gigantic Wheel at the corner of Coronation Street and Adelaide Street, *c.*1912. In what seems a desperate attempt to boost the flagging takings it was then labelled 'The Jolly Wheel'. Inside the entrance was a small bazaar.

88. *(bottom right)* The grounds of the Winter Gardens along Adelaide Street between the Big Wheel and the Empress Ballroom were laid out as Italian Gardens in 1896. They included a grotto at the eastern end. The Olympia Building now covers them.

89.  Blackpool at the beginning of the 20th century, showing a narrow and congested promenade before it was widened. Across the road, many of the gardens of South Beach have already been lost to stalls, the beginnings of the Golden Mile.

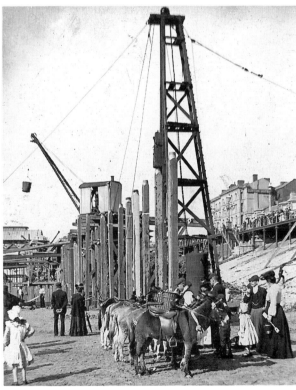

90. In March 1902, an ambitious promenade-widening scheme was started from South Shore, working northwards. This half of a stereoscopic view shows the initial stages of the construction of the new sea wall south of North Pier and gives a good impression of the area gained.

91.   A busy Corporation Street, then Lytham Street, is seen here from Church Street *c.*1908, with the town hall spire in the distance. On the left is the *Market Hotel*, built in 1880 to replace a beer house known as the *Market Inn*. It was once a favourite haunt of variety performer Florrie Forde. Beyond is the iron and glass St John's Market extension.

92.   St John's churchyard was closed for burials on 31 May 1873, following the opening of Layton cemetery. In the late 1920s the graves, excepting those of the Rev. W. Thornber and W.H. Cocker, were removed to Layton to allow for road widening. The railings in the photograph replaced a cobbled wall around the old church in 1862. Beyond can be seen shops on Abingdon Street.

93.  Four loaded waggonettes stand outside the *Clarence Hotel, c.*1905, from where visitors could depart on circular tours of the Fylde. Next door is Bannister's Bazaar, which had opened as the Borough Bazaar and Concert Hall in 1877. In 1928 the building became Feldman's Theatre, renamed the Queen's Theatre in November 1952. It was demolished 1972-3 for C&A's store.

94.   Imperial Terrace, Claremont Park, *c*.1905. The *Park Hotel* on the right had opened in the 1840s as the *Royal Edward* and was later the *Claremont Hotel*, when only the right two bays of it existed. By the 1920s it had become known by its present name, the *Carlton Hotel*. A streamlined sun lounge was added in 1937.

95.   The popularity of *Uncle Tom's Cabin* was such that a small fairground eventually developed there and lingered on after the *Cabin*'s demolition in 1908. On the right is the camera obscura, which had once stood on the cliff edge, and beyond it a tramcar passes one of the barns of Bank Farm.

96. E.H. Booth's reputation for quality was reflected in the elegant façade of the grocery store and café opened in Albert Terrace, north of Talbot Square, in 1905. Its size had been doubled in 1925. Booth had started his business in a converted barn in Market Street in 1847. The promenade premises were demolished in July 1972 and replaced by an unattractive cinema building.

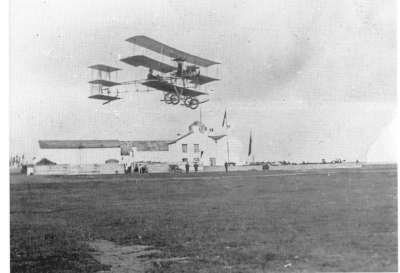

97. Blackpool has always been proud of its role in the development of aviation, On 18 October 1909, a month after the first flying meeting at Rheims, Blackpool staged one at Squires Gate, attracting the leading French aviators. Only one Briton, A.V. Roe, in his own aeroplane, managed to get airborne in a series of hops. Roe had more success at the 1910 Flying Carnival, where he is shown with Layton Hawes Farm behind.

98. On 1 August 1911, 20,000 people attended the opening meeting of the Clifton Park racecourse at Squires Gate, when the first race to be run was the £1,000 Coronation Gold Cup. Its success was short-lived and racing ended there in 1914. On 1 October 1915, the King's Lancashire Military Hospital opened on the site.

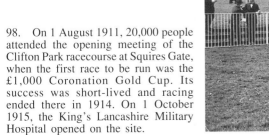

99.   In 1911, when the first Opera House was being enlarged, the Church Street façade of the Winter Gardens was rebuilt in a Renaissance style and clad in white faience. The existing iron and glass veranda was retained. When the Opera House was rebuilt in 1939, the façade was extended in the same style, although a modernist extension had been planned.

100. Blackpool's first small Opera House opened on 10 June 1889 with the D'Oyly Carte production of *The Yeomen of the Guard*. In 1911 it was remodelled as shown in the photograph. The present 3,000-seat theatre, designed in an art deco style by Charles Mackeith, opened on 14 July 1939 with George Formby in a revue called *Turned Out Nice Again*.

101. This elegant room was the foyer of the 1911 Opera House. Surprisingly, it still exists on the upper floor behind the Church Street façade of the Winter Gardens. However, it has lost some of its looks and is now seldom used.

102. Blackpool's first illuminations, in May and September 1912, were confined to Princess Parade, seen here. The following year, they were extended along the full length of the Promenade for the first time, only to be discontinued after 1914. It was in 1925 that autumn illuminations were re-introduced and, in 1930, tableaux were erected for the first time along the cliffs at Bispham.

103. The *Talbot Hotel*, with pebbled façade, was built by Thomas Clifton in 1845. From 1856 until 1921 it was owned by the Nickson family. Here, an enthusiastic crowd and mounted police await the arrival of Princess Louise at North station, opposite, on 1 May 1912. In January 1968 its site, next to the bus station, was cleared for offices.

104. Blackpool's mayor and mayoress, Councillor and Mrs. William Cartledge, with the Earl of Derby behind, pose outside the Town Hall among young men who are responding to the nation's call to arms. The group, photographed in November 1914 in front of patriotic posters, also includes Belgian soldiers.

105. Waterloo Road, South Shore's main shopping area, in the early 1920s looking east towards the old *Royal Oak Hotel* on Lytham Road. On the left is the former post office. The large block of shops was replaced with single-storey shops in the 1960s. On the extreme right are a few houses with gardens, now shops.

106.   At Hoo Hill, near the *Windmill Hotel*, Little Layton, the lanes from Bispham and Poulton converged by an old cottage known as Bunnock Hall. This photograph, taken in October 1922 looking east towards Wade's Farm, Little Carleton, shows the new Poulton Road under construction through the fields. The busy Plymouth Road roundabout was later built in the middle distance.

107.   The Blackpool Girls' Secondary School, Beech Avenue, was occupied in 1925, although the neo-classical building was only officially opened on 23 October 1928. From 1933 it was the Collegiate School for Girls until it merged with the boys' grammar school and moved to Highfurlong in 1971. It later became part of Knowle High School and was demolished in 1987 for flats.

108. The façade of the Tower building during the Carnival of 1923 or 24, when costume balls were held there. In the centre is depicted the once famous clown, Doodles, whose real name was William McAllister. He appeared at the Tower Circus between 1915 and 1944.

109.   The Open Air Baths, South Shore, were opened on 9 June 1923 at the start of the Carnival Week. Between the wars the baths featured in the autumn illuminations with tableaux representing Venice, Norway and the Wild West. Here the neo-classical café and entrance area is seen in 1937.

110.   The former popularity of the unheated South Shore Baths, once the world's largest, is demonstrated by this 1930s photograph. On 1 August 1927, 20,183 people were admitted and, on 13 October 1928, 27,465 people went there during the illumination display. However, declining attendances due to social changes and the public's expectations forced the baths' closure and subsequent demolition in February 1983.

111. An attraction in the Tower's roof gardens in 1927-30 was Midget Town, populated by Lester's midgets. They are posing here at the Country Club, where they played billiards and read newspapers. The 40-strong troupe also performed in the Tower Circus. The marriage of two of them at St Stephen's church was a well publicised event.

112. In February 1928, the Tower Company took over the Winter Gardens. A casualty was the Gigantic Wheel, which had been making a loss for many years. In November, its demolition began with the removal of the carriages, which were auctioned off and for many years could be seen dotted around the area as sheds and other outbuildings. One survives at Out Rawcliffe.

113.   Stanley Park, *c.*1930. Laid out to the design of Thomas H. and E. Prentice Mawson as an unemployment relief scheme, it was formally opened on 2 October 1926 by the 17th Earl of Derby and took his family name. Almost every amenity was put into the 250-acre site. An art deco café was added in 1936, all-weather pitches in the 1980s and, controversially, a sports centre in 1994.

114.   The Princess Street area became the home for Blackpool's utilities. The gas works opened there in 1854 and eventually spread beyond the railway. The electricity works, on the left, were opened by Lord Kelvin on 13 October 1893. In front of the gas holders in this 1936 photograph is Blundell Street tram depot, built in 1898 replacing the first tram shed of 1885.

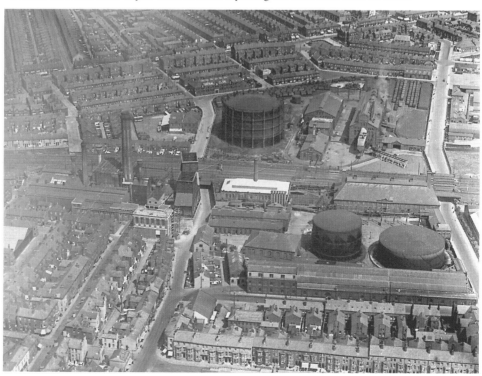

115.  Talbot Road bus station dates from 1923 when William Smith purchased Talbot Mews and his buses were allowed to stop there. In 1926, Blackpool Corporation acquired both the Mews and Smith's buses. The congested site was extended in February 1929 by the demolition of property as far as Cookson Street and the shelters in this 1930s photograph were then added.

116.  Blackpool's original destructor had opened in Rigby Road in 1885 and was rebuilt in 1903. In 1930 it was replaced by the one in the picture, on Bristol Avenue, Bispham. The photograph shows that much attention was given to its appearance. The destructor itself was demolished in December 1980 although the site is still a refuse collection point.

117.   The water tower, one of Blackpool's most prominent landmarks, is seen here under construction on Warbreck Hill in 1932. With its reservoir alongside, it provided better water pressure to the expanding town. Beside it, on Leys Road, are a cottage and a barn, remnants of the hamlet of Warbreck, which were pulled down shortly afterwards.

118. Blackpool's municipal aerodrome, east of Stanley Park, officially opened on 2 June 1931, but was never able to compete with Squires Gate, a better site. During the war, Bristol Beaufighters were serviced at Stanley Park and afterwards Hurricanes were scrapped there. Later it became a showground. The aerodrome's clubhouse and this hangar can still be seen at Blackpool Zoo, opened in 1975.

119. The *Grosvenor Hotel*, Cookson Street in August 1933. The building bears the date 1874 and the initials of George Ormerod, who owned several hotels in the Fylde. It was then called the *Raikes Hotel* but the name was changed *c.*1895, probably to avoid confusion with *Raikes Hall Hotel* in the nearby pleasure gardens.

120. The extraordinary exterior of the *Little Vic*, Victoria Street, a mixture of Spanish colonial and art deco styles, was created in 1933 when the *Victoria Inn*, originally part of the 1837 Victoria Promenade, was revamped by the architect, J.C. Derham. With its Spanish interior, modelled in plaster by Andrew Mazzei, it was arguably Blackpool's first 'theme pub'. It was demolished in 1989.

121. New offices for the *Gazette* and *Herald*, designed by Halstead Best, taking shape on Victoria Street in 1934. The adjacent *Trevelyan Hotel* was taken over by Gazette Stationers in 1947. After the *Gazette* had moved to premises on Preston New Road, the entire block was demolished for shops in 1987.

122. A film crew at work outside Luna Park, an amusement hall on the Golden Mile, on 5 June 1934. The building, originally neo-classical, was erected by William Read on South Beach in 1861 and housed a bazaar in the north wing, baths in the centre and assembly rooms to the south.

123. The interior of Luna Park in 1933. It included a guillotine illusion in which a girl was apparently decapitated and the severed head then answered questions. There was also a ghost train and in 1932 a Captain Varley wrestled with lions daily in a 'Den of Death'. Luna Park was pulled down in November 1967 and the Sea Life Centre is now there.

124. The forecourt of the Bee amusement arcade next to Tussaud's Waxworks on the Golden Mile in 1932. Among the slot machines are motorcycles in glass cases as competition prizes to lure people inside. On the left is one of Lawrence Wright's song booths.

125. The entrance to Central Pier in the mid-1930s still boasted a pavilion in an eastern style, which seemed to be obligatory to late Victorian and Edwardian pier buildings. The pavilion was replaced in 1967 by the bland Dixieland Bar, such domes and turrets then being considered irrelevant and even ugly.

126. Central Pier from the pavilion, *c.*1935. On the left is one of the hallmarks of the period, a song booth. In the 1980s the pier was enlivened by bright post-modernist arcades and in April 1990 a 108ft. diameter wheel was erected on it.

127.   The Boots fire of 7 October 1936 not only destroyed the store but also the municipal offices above, although most of the town's records and plans were saved. A Blackpool fireman, Raymond Laycock, who had married only days before, died during the blaze. A fire appliance is seen here in West Street opposite the market, with Birley Street beyond.

128. Looking along Central Drive towards the Palatine building from the vicinity of Vance Road in 1936. In 1938, the property advertising Lawrence Wright's songs was rebuilt as the *Castle Hotel*, the licence being transferred from the *Castle Inn* on Market Street. The road, then as now, was entirely given over to the holiday industry,

129. The *Commercial Hotel* on Waterloo Road, South Shore, is shown here in the early 1930s before it was replaced by the *Dutton Arms* erected on the site of the boarding houses on the Promenade beyond. Behind the railings in the foreground had stood West House, built in the 1830s by Thomas Moore, the founder of South Shore.

130. Built on the site of Woolworth's bazaar and the *Royal Hotel*, Woolworth's superstore on the Promenade is shown taking shape on 20 November 1936. Its clock tower was completed many months later. The building was destined to become one of Blackpool's most familiar landmarks, if only for its proximity to the Tower. It is now one of a dwindling number of the town's art deco buildings in cream faience.

131. Lockhart's Café at the corner of Bank Hey Street and Adelaide Street, shortly after being rebuilt in the modernist style. Next to it, work continues on the last extension to R.H.O. Hill's department store, completed in 1937. Inevitably for the time, both buildings were faced in cream tiles. Hill's was destroyed by fire in 1967.

132. The imposing neo-classical façade of the Co-operative Emporium, *c.*1938. It was erected on Coronation Street in 1936, next to a Co-op store built in 1929 on Albert Road. By the 1980s trade had dwindled and the site was cleared in 1989 for a planned shopping centre. This failed, leaving a hole in the ground which was eventually filled in to form a car park.

133. The Co-operative Emporium even had its own theatre known as the Jubilee Theatre. At one time films were shown there. The proscenium frieze was removed prior to demolition and was displayed for a while at Cyril Critchlow's nearby museum of entertainment, which had an even smaller theatre.

134. Talbot Road bus station, with car park above, nearing completion in 1939 and clad in tiles of cream and green, matching the buses. High above Talbot Road was a frieze depicting the progress of transport. In May 1963, the building was re-clad in grey painted corrugated steel, losing what architectural merit it had in the process.

135. The prestigious Derby Baths on the Promenade and Warley Road opened in July 1939. After the war, water shows were staged and later international swimming competitions there were often televised. During the 1980s, falling attendances and high maintenance costs led to the baths' closure and their controversial demolition in March 1990.

136. This photograph, taken in February 1960 from Dickson Road, shows the exterior of Derby Baths' remedial wing as originally completed in faience. The section was opened as late as 1965, having been re-clad in grey corrugated steel, thereby losing the architectural unity of the baths.

137.   A deserted Central station in December 1938. The line between Hounds Hill and Lytham had opened on 6 April 1863. In 1899 the original station was replaced by that in the photograph. It was completed along with excursion platforms for Easter 1901. After the station's closure in 1964, the building was used for bingo until its demolition in January 1974.

138.   Wilkinson's, photographed c.1938, was one of two yards on the east side of Bonny Street near Central station, of which the platform canopies can be seen beyond. The buildings in the area, which were cleared c.1959, dated from the 1840s, with the entrance to the other yard, Pleasant View, having a stone lintel inscribed 'John Bonny 1848'.

139.   Old property on Church Street awaiting demolition in 1939. A large building to include a shopping arcade, offices and an underground car park was due to be erected on the site but the Second World War intervened. The site was used as an open air market and a car park until British Home Stores was built there, opening in 1957.

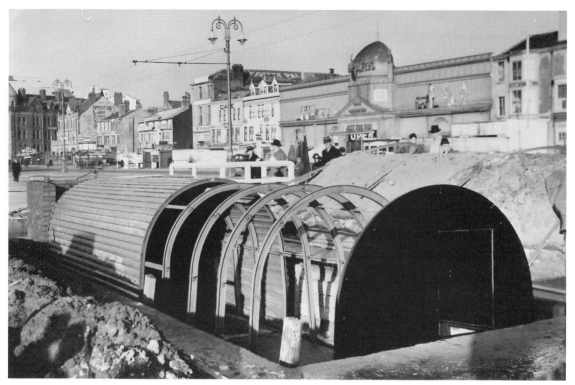

140.  The construction of an air raid shelter on the Promenade opposite the Golden Mile in 1939. Large concrete blocks were also placed there to thwart an invasion and ferro-concrete posts protruded from the sands to prevent aircraft landing safely.

141.   Blackpool suffered relatively little damage from bombing during the war. However, on 12 September 1940, a German plane swept down on North station dropping bombs. Nearby Seed Street took the brunt of the attack, and eight people were killed and 14 injured. The remaining terraced houses in the street were eventually cleared away by the council for car parking.

142.   In 1940 a huge aircraft factory was built at Squires Gate, along with three runways which necessitated the closure of St Annes Road beyond the *Halfway House*. Wellington bombers were assembled there. In the photograph, workers pose with the last one built at the subsidiary plant at Stanley Park Aerodrome.

143. *(top left)* Talbot Square, *c.*1950. The Victorian cast-iron fountain of 1870 had been incorporated in a bus and tram shelter *c.*1920. However, in the 1930s the shelter was superseded by one with classical columns, which lasted until the 1960s. The Town Hall, completed in 1900, is seen with its spire which was removed in 1966.

144. *(left)* Manchester Square, formed by the junction of Lytham Road and the Promenade, is close to where Spen Dyke (the black pool), now culverted, flows into the sea. The original public house had been built there *c.*1850. In 1936 it was replaced by this striking modernist hotel, designed by J.C. Derham, which was altered in the 1960s.

145. *(above)* The semi-rural Blowing Sands area of Marton in June 1954, just before 'improvements' to Common Edge Road. It has since suffered from the impact of housing development and traffic. The foreground is to be the site of a large roundabout on the M55 to Squires Gate link road, started in February 1994. The listed white cottage will survive as an anachronism.

146.   The Winter Gardens during the first Royal Command Variety Performance to take place outside London, on 13 April 1955 at the Opera House. There, the Queen and the Duke of Edinburgh were entertained by such stars as Eddie Fisher, Jewel and Warriss, Alma Cogan, Al Read, Charlie Caroli, Albert Modley and George Formby. A royal box had been constructed for the occasion.

147.   Lane's amusement arcade on the Golden Mile was also known as Fairyland. The building, which replaced the original 1904 Fairyland destroyed by fire on 20 July 1931, contained 10 tableaux with over 200 figures of fairies, elves and dragons. It was demolished in November 1970 to allow the widening of Chapel Street.

148.   Talbot Road, *c.*1960. Next to the 1894 octagonal extension of Sacred Heart church is Bateson's furnishers in premises built in 1859 as Viener's Bazaar. Adjoining it is the presbytery of Sacred Heart, since rebuilt and extended up to the *Railway Hotel* on the right.

149.   Photographed in the 1950s, Victoria Street has, since the mid-1970s, been transformed by pedestrianisation and shopping developments, some partially obscuring the arch of the Winter Gardens beyond. A surprising survivor is the building on the left, which opened in 1837 as the Victoria Promenade, Blackpool's first public assembly hall.

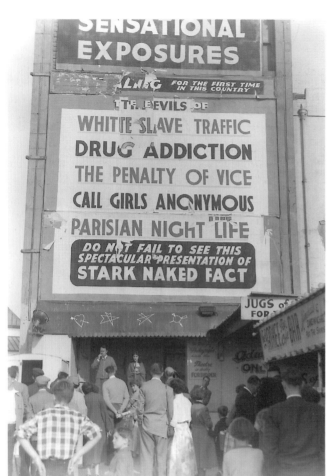

150a & b. Chard's went under the name of 'The Montmartre Theatre' in the 1950s. Inside, a scene of living art deco is revealed to the audience by a bereted Stanley Callanan, for many years a barker there.

151.   The Golden Mile achieved notoriety with Luke Gannon's side shows in the 1930s. In the 1950s it was at its sleaziest with attractions like 'The Palace of Strange Girls'. Shown here in 1965 shortly before its demolition, the façade of Chard's theatre, a building which had been the earnest British Workman dining rooms in the 1880s, has descended into hell and kitsch.

152.   The approach to Central station *c*.1960 which saw, at the height of the season, over a hundred trains a day. The line closed on 1 November 1964 and now coach and car parks predominate. On the right is Blackpool Football Club's ground with a canopy under construction over the kop. The photograph was taken from one of the floodlight pylons, added in 1958.

153a & b.   How the corner of Abingdon Street and Church Street was transformed *c*.1958. Property dating from the 1860s was replaced by a stylish building faced in black mosaic lined with pink. It contained Paige's ladies fashion store, Boston Man's Shop and a shoe shop. In the 1980s, the Next group took over most of the building and covered the mosaic with ivory paint.

154. The distinctive Lewis's store, with its white honeycomb and pale blue tiled façade, opened on 2 April 1964 where the Palace and the *County Hotel* had once stood. Following Lewis's closure on 9 January 1993, the cladding and two storeys were removed in its transformation to a neo-classical building in 1994, with Woolworth's as the main trader.

155. The Empire, Church Street, opened on 4 July 1895. Unsuccessful, it was sold in 1900, re-opening as the Hippodrome. By 1910 it was regularly showing films and in 1929 it was taken over by ABC. Live shows continued to be staged during the summer season. Virtually rebuilt as the ABC Theatre in 1962-3, it is now the MGM Cinema.

156a & b.  The Golden Mile in the 1960s, before old buildings and the hotch-potch of stalls gave way to monotonous modern amusement halls. However, more recently, these too have changed and the Golden Mile is today more colourful than ever before. On the left of the first view is the *New Inn and Central Hotel* where Coral Island now stands.

157. The box-like Mecca Ballroom, Central Drive, was considered a stylish building when it opened in 1965. Its popularity eventually declined, being unable to compete against discos and nightclubs, and it closed in October 1981. The Top Rank Bowl had closed in May 1970 but re-opened as the Commonwealth Sports Club in April 1978. In April 1990 it became the Premier Bowl.

158. A 1965 scheme to redevelop the centre of Blackpool featured tiered promenades and high-rise buildings. Since then, much of the town centre has been rebuilt, though mainly in a piecemeal manner and not as envisaged in the model. A single concrete bridge was erected across the promenade in 1975, but its demolition is planned as part of a period restoration of the sea front.

159.	Adelaide Street in 1976, showing the United Methodist Free church of 1864. On 13 May 1894 it became the first local church to be illuminated by electricity. Nearly everything in the photograph was cleared away for the Hounds Hill Centre, built across Adelaide Street at this spot and officially opened 29 August 1980.

160.	Ibbison Street, part of the Revoe district, is seen here from the *George Hotel*, Central Drive. The terraced houses were cleared away in 1974 and replaced by the sheltered housing of Ibbison Court.

# The Pleasure Beach

161.   South Shore's fairground about the time it became officially called the Pleasure Beach in 1906. The once solitary *Star Inn* caters for those attracted to the assortment of rides and stalls. Beyond is the switchback railway, reputedly on the site since the early 1890s. The Gypsies' tents and caravans are clustered nearby. By early 1910 they had all been encouraged to leave.

162. On 1 August 1904, Sir Hiram Maxim's Captive Flying Machine opened on the fairground which had been developing on the beach at South Shore south of Victoria Pier. It still runs to this day on the Pleasure Beach and its original machinery can be viewed through glass. The aerodynamic gondolas, suspended beneath arrows, have been replaced with rocket ships.

163. By 1911 the stalls along the shoreline had been consolidated to form 'Spanish Street'. Here in 1912, although very much the same, it had become 'Ye Olde Englishe Street'. To quote a contemporary guide, 'Where formerly stood the picturesque casas of Spain, there are now faithful replicas of domestic dwellings of the Elizabethan and other periods'.

164. In 1919 thousands of visitors were able to enjoy the novel experience of flying when the Avro company operated pleasure flights from the sands at South Shore. During the same summer months, Avro ran an air service between Manchester, Southport and Blackpool. Here, coming in to land, an Avro 504K passes the old switchback railway and the Naval Spectatorium.

165. An illuminated Pleasure Beach during a September evening in 1912, showing the Lighthouse Helter Skelter of 1905, Thompson's Scenic Railway, opened June 1907, and the Rainbow Wheel of 1912. The latter lasted until 1934.

166. The Pleasure Beach's response to the roller-skating craze, c.1909, was to build the resort's largest rink, seen here in mock-Tudor guise in 1926. It was also used as an exhibition hall, an industrial exhibition being held there in 1912. The building was replaced by the Ice Drome which opened in 1937.

167a & b.   The art deco style Novelty Cinema of 1933, in a building opened the year before as a news theatre. Later in the decade it became the Cresta Tea-room and the fountain was modernised with glass bricks. Next to the cinema was this camera-shaped photographic booth.

168. An evening view of the Pleasure Beach in 1936. The Noah's Ark of 1922 has been modernised and 'futuristic' animals added. Unfortunately, being made of wood and hardboard, these strange mutations eventually rotted and were superseded by evolutionary throwbacks in 1961.

169. Arguably the finest example of the 1930s 'Brave New World' architecture was Emberton's station for the Pleasure Beach Express, rebuilt after a fire on 18 July 1934. It is seen here with the 1933 Roller Coaster's entrance behind. The station was altered *c*.1960 and, in 1970, rebuilt as a Victorian station, in a world no longer quite as brave.

170. The River Caves on the Pleasure Beach have taken several forms since their introduction in 1905 and the boat journey through strange lands is still an atmospheric experience today. It is seen here in the 1930s.

171. In 1937 the River Caves were also given the modernist treatment, in what might be described as a toytown cubist style. In the 1950s they were re-modelled with simulated Aztec rock carvings.

172. The Pleasure Beach's architectural flagship of the 1930s was the Casino, which replaced a 'wedding cake' styled building of 1913. Designed by Joseph Emberton assisted by the local architect, Halstead Best, it is seen here nearing completion in 1939. Some of its original character was lost when it was converted into the Wonderful World building in 1978.

173. Blackpool Pleasure Beach's awe-inspiring 235ft. high roller-coaster rises above the imitation of the old Casino on 'Ocean Boulevard' and the *Star Hotel* on 12 February 1994. The ride opened to the public on 28 May 1994. It symbolises the continuing investment in Blackpool as a resort and the ride's intended name, 'The Pepsi-Max Big One', is itself a sign of the times.

# Bibliography

Aspin, C., *Dizzy Heights, The Story of Lancashire's First Flying Men* (1988).

Blackpool & Fylde Historical Society, *Blackpool's Progress, Jubilee Year, 1926*, 2nd edition (1990)

Cunliffe, N., *Uncle Tom's Cabin* (1982).

Dougill, D., *Blackpool's Buses* (1982).

Edmondson, I., *Art Deco Blackpool* (unpublished).

France, R.S., 'Layton Hawes and Marton Mere', *The Fylde Historical & Antiquarian Society*, vol. 1 (1940).

Hornsey, B., 'Cinemas of Blackpool', *Mercia Bioscope*, issue 49 (1993).

Hutton, W., *A Description of Blackpool in 1788* (reprinted 1944).

Lightbown, T. & Wood, A.W., *Blackpool in Old Picture Postcards*, vol. 2 (1990).

Marshall, J., *The Lancashire & Yorkshire Railway* (1969).

Smith, W.J., 'Blackpool: A Sketch of its Growth, 1740-1851', *Transactions of the Lancashire and Cheshire Antiquarian Society*, vol. 69 (1959).

Stott, A., *Layton Village* (1980).

Thornber, W., *The History of Blackpool and its Neighbourhood* (1837, reprinted 1985).

Turner, B. & Palmer, S., *The Blackpool Story*, 1st edn. (1976).

Wood, A.W. & Lightbown, T., *Blackpool in Old Picture Postcards* (1983).